100 IDEAS
FOR SURVIVING
YOUR FIRST YEAR
IN TEACHING

CONTINUUM ONE HUNDREDS SERIES

100 Ideas for Managing Behaviour – Johnnie Young

100 Ideas for Supply Teachers – Julia Murphy

100 Ideas for Surviving Your First Year in Teaching – Laura-Jane Fisher

100 Ideas for Teaching Citizenship – Ian Davies

100 Ideas for Teaching Creativity – Stephen Bowkett

100 Ideas for Teaching English – Angella Cooze

100 Ideas for Teaching History – Julia Murphy

100 Ideas for Teaching Languages – Nia Griffith

100 Ideas for Teaching Mathematics – Mike Ollerton

100 Ideas for Teaching Science – Sharon Archer

100 Ideas for Teaching Thinking Skills – Stephen Bowkett

100 Ideas for Trainee Teachers – Angella Cooze

100 IDEAS
FOR SURVIVING
YOUR FIRST
YEAR IN
TEACHING

Laura-Jane Fisher

continuum
LONDON • NEW YORK

Continuum International Publishing Group

The Tower Building   15 East 26th Street
11 York Road   New York, NY 10010
London
SE1 7NX

www.continuumbooks.com

British Library Cataloguing-in-Publication Data
A catalogue record for this book is available from the
British Library.

ISBN: 0–8264–8667–3 (paperback)

Library of Congress Cataloging-in-Publication Data
A catalog record for this book is available from the
Library of Congress

Typeset by Ben Cracknell Studios
Printed and bound in Great Britain by MPG Books Ltd,
Bodmin, Cornwall

This book is dedicated to my Mother, Frances,
and Dad, Malcolm, who helped me through
what was the hardest year of teaching.
Thank you.

CONTENTS

ACKNOWLEDGEMENTS   xii
PREFACE   xiii

SECTION 1   **Finishing off your training**

1	Finding the right job	2
2	Understanding job adverts	4
3	The application	5
4	The interview	6
5	The lesson to impress	7
6	Rejection	8
7	Getting the job	9

SECTION 2   **Preparation**

8	The long summer	12
9	What you should do in August (on top of sunbathing)	14
10	Planning lessons over the summer: dos and don'ts	15
11	Visiting the school	16

SECTION 3   **The first week**

12	The night before the first day	18
13	The first day	19
14	Getting there in one piece	20
15	Finding your feet and making them go in the right direction	21
16	First impressions	22
17	All those papers	23
18	Your little black book (mine's A4 actually)	24
19	Using your position of power	25
20	Revealing too much of yourself	26
21	Professional boundaries	27

SECTION 4 The support system

22 Your mentor 30

23 The head of new teachers 31

24 Colleagues 32

SECTION 5 Classroom management

25 Resources 34

26 Corridors 35

27 The first telling off 36

28 Consistency 37

29 Sanctions and rewards 38

30 Setting the boundaries 39

31 Your classroom layout 40

32 Five golden rules of behaviour management 41

33 Personal safety 42

34 Child protection 43

35 The problem child 44

36 The problem class 45

37 Involving pupils 46

38 From the parents' view 47

39 Passing the buck 48

40 Getting help 49

41 Never let them see you cry 50

SECTION 6 The new kid on the block

42 Passing your first year 52

43 That bad observation 53

44 Making your mark 54

45 Use your youth 56

46	Remember your schooldays	57
47	Beyond the call of duty	58
48	Just because you're new doesn't mean you're wrong	59
49	Be outrageous	60

SECTION 7 The reality of being a teacher

50	Meetings	62
51	Reports	63
52	Timing	64
53	Timetable	65
54	The difference between a tick and marking	66
55	ICT can be your worst enemy	68
56	Parents' evenings	69
57	Your bag	70
58	Your desk	71
59	Your classroom	72
60	Staffroom gossip	73
61	Your 'to do' pile	74
62	Exam pressure	75
63	A bit wacky	76
64	Your memory	77
65	Break time	78
66	Bus duty	79
67	The pay cheque	80
68	Mid-week despair	81
69	Fridays are sacred	82
70	Sunday blues	83
71	Time off	84

SECTION 8 **Life as a teacher**

72	Dealing with stress	86
73	Having a life outside work	87
74	Beauty sleep	88
75	Start your day the right way	89
76	Dressing like a teacher	90
77	12 reports, 2 parents' evenings, 4 meetings, 70 books to mark and it's only Wednesday	91
78	I've got a headache, I'm coughing and sneezing – I'll go to school	92
79	A Mars bar and water make lunch	93
80	Looking after yourself all day	94
81	Making mistakes	96
82	The day you want to give up	97
83	Those days when you can't teach	98
84	Sharing your day	99
85	Talking shop	100

SECTION 9 **The eternal student**

86	Courses	102
87	Your subject, your learning	103
88	Videoing yourself	104
89	Self-assessment	105
90	Keep reading	106
91	Other sources of information	107
92	Admit your weaknesses	108
93	Make your strengths clear	109

SECTION 10 **One year down, another 44 (at least) to go**

94	July	112
95	Do you still want to be a teacher?	113
96	Are you in the right school for you?	114
97	Applying for your second post	115
98	This time you know what's coming	116
99	The rest of your life as a teacher	117
100	And finally . . .	118

ACKNOWLEDGEMENTS

Thanks to all those at Continuum who have helped me with my first book and to those who taught me first at Lawnswood High School, Leeds and then at Liverpool Hope. Many thanks also to Bingley Grammar, Bradford who gave me my first teaching job.

At the end of my first year of teaching I looked back and wished I had known one hundred things at the beginning of the year that I knew at the end. These were the things that I wasn't taught at university or college.

Although I can't promise you'll read this and fly through your first year of teaching, it at least holds practical hints and tips that will help you along the way. Some of the ideas are taken from my own experience of what went really well and others are taken from the things I did badly and therefore learnt invaluable lessons from. By reading this you shouldn't make the mistakes I did, and even if you do at least you'll realize you're not the only one!

Laura-Jane Fisher

Finishing off your training

The key to finding the right job is not to settle for the first thing that comes up. People have a habit of panicking around Easter if they haven't got a job. Don't. There will always be someone who gets a job really early on in the year – I think one of our students got a job in November – but it's more important to get the right job than it is to get just any job.

The best place to look for jobs is in *The Times Educational Supplement*, which is published each Thursday. It also has a website that is updated regularly, www.tes.co.uk. All major papers have an education section with jobs advertised – the *Guardian* is particularly good and has a companion website, www.jobs.guardian.co.uk. This makes it quick and easy to see what's on offer.

When looking for a job the first thing most people focus on is the location. Pick a city or town that you want to live in, then get a map and circle how far you are willing to travel. This will give you a number of places within your travelling distance.

After finding a school where you want to live, look at what sort of school it is – is it inner city or rural? These schools are very different. Inner-city schools will usually be multicultural and have a large catchment area, rural schools are more often than not predominantly white British.

Next, check out the school:

○ Look at its website.
○ What are the grades like?
○ Look at its Ofsted report by checking the government website, www.ofsted.gov.uk

Check out the catchment area:

○ Go to the school when the final bell rings. What are the pupils like coming out – loud and hyperactive, or friendly?
○ Watch them around the streets. Go and buy a packet of crisps at the local shop they go into – what are they like with members of the public?
○ Even ask the shopkeeper what the children are like.

○ Also look at the houses: are they big and grand or is there poverty in the area?

All this can tell you a lot about the pupils before you've even stepped into a classroom.

As teachers become more expensive, schools deal with this by doubling up on what their staff teach. You can therefore expect to teach subjects that were not part of your training, such as general studies at A level, PSHE and citizenship. Humanity teachers are often expected to teach geography, history and RE even though they may have a degree in history. English teachers are asked to teach drama all the time and science teachers are even asked to teach PE. Look carefully at what the job description is. You will often be sent a list of what characteristics and skills are compulsory and what are desirable. It might say 'have a degree in English' in the compulsory section but it might also say 'willing to teach media and drama' is desirable. If so, check what you will be required to teach and think about what you want to teach. Taking on a whole new subject is never an easy task, particularly when you are still new to teaching.

The application is the most important part of getting a job. It must be right. The best thing to do is get as much advice as possible. Do a draft, then show it to your lecturers at university and the teachers at your placement school. I even asked the deputy head who was in charge of hiring to read mine and asked him, 'Would you give me a job?' He was able to tell me what he looked for in an application and the most useful thing told me was to grab their attention in the first paragraph of your covering letter – after all, those hiring will be reading dozens of letters and if they are not impressed straight away they won't read the rest of what you have to say.

Don't forget that the application has to convey your true self so be honest and make sure it shows a bit of your personality – after all it's you who's going for the job.

Mention:

○ What experiences you've had.
○ What you will do to help promote their school ethos as it stands.
○ What you would bring to their school.
○ What interests you have outside school – remember they don't want a teaching robot, they want a fully rounded person. These skills can be used in school and in the community so if you volunteer at a hospital, or sing for charity then highlight this. Teachers with special skills make for good public relations for their school!

The interview is only one part of the recruitment process, on top of this you will have to teach a lesson and probably meet some of the pupils. However, the interview is a wonderful opportunity not only to show yourself off but to review what the school is like and exactly what job you're getting yourself into.

Below is a collection of the sort of questions you'll be asked, so think about them before the interview and have some great answers up your sleeve:

o Why have you chosen this school?
o Why did you pick this subject?
o Why is your subject important to a child's development?
o What and why is your favourite book/scientist/sport? (Depending on the subject.)
o What would you do if you had a child misbehaving in your class?
o Why is a tutor important?
o What was the best lesson you have ever given?
o What was the worst lesson you have ever given? (Tip: make sure you know why it was wrong and how you improved it!)

Always take time answering the questions and make sure you understand what they are asking. If you need them to repeat it then ask.

Don't forget to have a list of questions you want to ask them, for example:

o What importance do you place on extra-curricular activities?
o Are you connected to any federations?
o What will my duties be?

But remember, don't lie in the interview, be yourself. If they don't take you as a result of the answers you give then that is not the school for you.

The school will often send you a theme or subject that they want you to teach a 20-minute lesson on, to a selected group of children. Don't panic – you do lessons every day. Plan the lesson out as you have been taught and get copies so you can hand them to your observers, but then put yours down. If you stray from the plan don't panic – it happens in teaching and will give you something to talk about when you are reviewing the lesson in your interview.

If possible try out the lesson at your placement school and be honest – tell the students you are going for an interview and ask them, 'Did you like the lesson? How would you change it?' After all, pupils' reactions are the best feedback.

But most importantly see it as an opportunity to show what you can do. Even do something outrageous – I had Year 9 boys standing on desks reading 'To be or not to be'. Try to get noticed. They will probably have five other candidates doing exactly the same subject and you want yours to stand out. Use everything from music to costume to visual aids. Enjoy it and show them something of yourself.

REJECTION

I have never found anyone who got the first job they went for. When it comes down to it not every job is for you, nor every school for that matter. Sometimes the school might reject you and sometimes you reject the school. But the important thing about rejection is that you can learn from it.

All schools will give you feedback on your lesson and interview, take this feedback – even though it may be the last thing you want to do – and review it for next time. Make a list of the questions you were asked, particularly the ones that you couldn't answer or those you found difficult. Spend time going through them, write out your answers and ask your lecturers and teachers at your placement how they would have approached them.

One of the great things about teaching is that 9 out of 10 times they will tell you on the spot whether or not you have the job. You'll all be in one room and the deputy head will come in and take one person out, and that person has the job. If it's you, well done!

They will now start to give you information that you will need to know for the following September. But you're still thinking 'Oh wow I have a job!' and will find it difficult to take anything in. Try your best to focus. You may well need to do some paperwork and such things as swapping telephone numbers with the head of department so they can contact you if they need to. If you're lucky the head of department will take you to one side and give you a chance to get your head together and do what needs to be done. Of course, when all this is out of the way go out and celebrate. Go into school with a headache for one day, no one will blame you. Do easy lessons for once! Then focus on passing your teaching course.

Preparation

THE LONG SUMMER

One of the few good things about working towards a teaching certificate is that you finish in early June. By this time if you're lucky – and believe me it has a lot to do with luck – you'll have a job. But with this job comes the worry of September. What do I teach? What do I wear? Suddenly you are aware that for the first time in your life you will walk into a class by yourself and teach a lesson. This is where the fear sets in, and people deal with it in different ways.

One person might think, 'It'll be all right as long as I plan everything.' This is the sort of person who will plan lessons all summer on what they think they might be teaching. Will write dozens of lists that will eventually be lost and will pace up and down the stairs at Waterstones looking for anything that may help them in September. In reality, you'll only read a fraction of the books you buy, you'll use either a couple or none of your lesson plans and you'll be so tired by September you'll be counting the days till half-term.

The next person thinks 'It'll be fine as long as I don't think about it.' This person will do no work for the first five weeks, will hardly sleep (because they'll be having nightmares about their first day) and in a last-minute panic will try to read and plan everything in the final two weeks of freedom they have left. This person wastes the money they spend on their holiday because they go away for two weeks and worry about school, get nothing organized and realize on the first day of school they don't have any clothes that don't say 'Fcuk' on the front. Finally there is the person who falls neatly in between these two, which as you can gather is the ideal way to be. By the way, this is not the one I was. I fell into the first category and still have the untouched lesson plans to prove it! So:

○ Make sure you know what you're teaching in the first week.
○ Think about how you're going to introduce yourself to the pupils.

○ Think about what to wear. You need to look less like a student and more like a teacher, especially if you are teaching A-level – those 'children' might be only six years younger than you.

○ Think about what regulations you want in your classroom and stick to them (deciding this now will make for an easier start to the year).

WHAT YOU SHOULD DO IN AUGUST
(ON TOP OF SUNBATHING)

Teacher training is hard, plain and simple. So the first thing you must do is take some time off – even if you don't go away make sure you put your work aside for at least a week.

Then, before school finishes, get in touch with your head of department, go in and see them or just have a phone conversation. Plan beforehand what you need to ask them, even the questions you think are silly. I asked where the nearest toilet was. Well, it was important to me! They will have schemes of work for you; these can be taken home and looked over well before your September deadline. Then read some of the books you bought on your course, because I just know you didn't read them all when you were studying! Oh – and make sure you work on your tan at the same time, and have plenty of breaks. I found one chapter and a two-hour film a good balance. Also concentrate on books that talk about classroom management – they'll be the most useful. This is the only preparation you can do as far as work goes so enjoy the sun, enjoy daytime TV, because it isn't going to last long.

It is unusual, but not unheard of, for new teachers to be asked to put together some schemes of work, maybe for your GCSE group. If you are required to do this, you need to do several things:

1 Make the first two weeks a bit of fun. Don't forget they will be judging you, so don't give them a 12-page essay on the first day. Pupils like teachers who understand their workload.
2 Give them something that will enable you to assess them on a basic level, but not a test – that won't make you popular!
3 Don't set them work that will take lots of marking. The first couple of weeks are tiring and there is a lot of paperwork to do anyway, so don't add to it.
4 You will be given schemes of work for lower years – don't follow them religiously, try to bring your own personality to them.

Don't:

1 Plan in minute detail for the first term – you don't know them and they don't know you, so this will just waste time and energy.
2 Teach things you are unsure of in the first week; stick with something you know, it will give you confidence.
3 Set any homework. All schools will have a homework timetable, so find that first.
4 You won't always be able to plan lessons as you did at university, nor will you need to. Work out a shorter way of planning. Don't keep writing three sheets for each lesson.

PLANNING LESSONS OVER THE SUMMER: DOS AND DON'TS

VISITING THE SCHOOL

It's always worth if possible visiting the school before the start of term; if you are able to familiarize yourself a bit you'll find you're less nervous on the first day. You need to make a note of the following things:

○ Which door do you come in? Is there a code for this door?
○ Where is the staffroom?
○ Where is your nearest toilet? Staff and pupils' toilets.
○ Where is your classroom? If you don't have one of your own, where are your subject rooms?
○ Where does your head of department/faculty teach?
○ Where is the nurse's office?
○ Where are the head of year or house offices?
○ Where are the head and the deputy's office?

Get all this jotted down because it's information you will need all year round. Although visiting a school is a good idea, doing supply work there is not. Some schools will offer you this and I know it is tempting on the money side but it's better for you to do supply work elsewhere instead, so if you can get out of it do so.

The first week

THE NIGHT BEFORE THE FIRST DAY

Don't leave anything unprepared for your first morning at school (this goes for the whole year as well). You would not believe how quickly that morning will go so make sure you organize everything the night before. Decide what you are going to wear and stick to it. Check your bag – you should have plenty of water, lunch, a notepad to write things down so you don't forget, plenty of pens and pencils and body spray!

Try not to think about the first day. Easier to say than do, I know – but you don't know what is going to happen so there is no point making up scenarios. Do something to take your mind off it, but by this I don't mean go out and drink yourself silly. A headache in the morning will not help. Have dinner somewhere nice, go out with friends or go to the cinema and then make sure you get home and to bed at a sensible time. You might think you're so nervous you won't sleep but at least being in bed will help you rest. And set your alarm for that little bit earlier, you'll need it.

For any child the first day of school involves a lot of tears and insecurity. The first day for new teachers is exactly the same. However it is the worst day – and it only lasts 24 hours.

Stay calm about it. Remember no one expects you to get it right the first time and there will be plenty of people around to help, just ask. There is usually a training day at the beginning of term, so make a list of what you need to find out:

o What is your timetable and will it change?
o Where are your first classes?
o Where are the resources?
o When will you get your class list and special educational needs (SEN) information?

Try to stick with your head of department, that way you won't get lost and they will help by introducing you around. During the first staff meeting they will usually introduce new teachers/staff. Write their names down and spot where they are in the hall. We had to stand up and wave (makes you feel like a right fool). Then at the end of the meeting head for the other new teachers, introduce yourself, find out where their department is. They are the best people to know as they will be having the same worries and stumbling blocks – arrange to meet up for lunch or drinks after work.

GETTING THERE IN ONE PIECE

I have always worried about being late for things, and the one thing you don't want to do is be late on your first day. So plan out your journey to work, do a test run – and make sure you do it on a weekday at the time you would be leaving, as traffic changes. Then leave ten minutes early anyway.

If you have an office job and you are five minutes late because a train doesn't come or there is a crash on the road it doesn't matter as much, but for a teacher who has a Year 7 class first, being five minutes late can be catastrophic. Carry a mobile and if you're going to be late inform the school that your class must be covered.

Most schools start the year with a training day, which is perfect for easing you into a new school. I'll give you the same advice that I have just given my Year 7 tutor group – and that is to take your timetable and find out where all your rooms are before classes start. I spent the first week of school asking the children where certain rooms were – they found it hilarious and I found it an embarrassing necessity. Not to mention that there will always be a child who thinks it's amusing to send you to the chemistry department when you are looking for geography.

FINDING YOUR FEET AND MAKING THEM GO IN THE RIGHT DIRECTION

I was always told at university that first impressions are vitally important for a teacher when they are meeting a class for the first time. This is simply not the case. Children have very little memory when it comes to school and, although this might be harsh, the fact that you messed up one lesson will be nowhere near as interesting as the text message your Year 11 are passing round!

However you do have to decide how you are going to handle your group, because consistency will help you out. There are teachers who tell you to go into a class and be strict right from the beginning, get control of the class right away and they won't give you any trouble. You can do this, it does work, but there needs to be a balance. A lot of pupils hate teachers because of what they stand for: authority, rules, discipline – prison wardens are the same. Teachers are human! Would it be so bad if the pupils knew that? So set down your rules and expectations for your pupils and yourself and then show your human side. Don't stand rigid in front of the class, perch on something – you'll look more relaxed. Show interest in what you are teaching, after all it is your subject. Make sure you change the tone of your voice. And it's OK to admit to them that you might have had a bad day.

After my first week a teacher I hardly knew came up to me in the corridor and said that I taught her godson English. Horror! What had he said about me? Something dreadful? Accused me of being the worst teacher in the world? He had said I was 'strict but cool'. There can be no better compliment for a teacher.

A school is built on its memos. You get memos for everything. Not all will be of use to you but as a new teacher you won't know that. In fact there will be some pieces of paper you think are completely useless until it gets to July and you realize you need those little numbers on that obscure piece of paper you vaguely remembering seeing in September. So you have to track it down, almost an impossible task in a school. You have to find out who distributed it, then find out their number or school location, then spend three weeks chasing someone down when you don't even know what they look like.

To save yourself from this, keep it *all*. Get a thick folder, and call it 'bits and bobs'. Use this folder to house *every* piece of paper that you are given in the first two weeks. Don't in this period of time try to put things into any sort of order or category. Sure it might seem logical that a SEN report on a child would go in your SEN file, but how logical do you think schools are? It might in fact need to go into your class file or work file or even your differentiation file. So keep everything together and give yourself a chance to work out how the school operates and where these different pieces of paper will be most useful. *Never* get rid of your bits and bobs file, there are always pieces of paper that just don't have a home.

ALL THOSE PAPERS

YOUR LITTLE BLACK BOOK (MINE'S A4 ACTUALLY)

Not all the information you get in the first couple of weeks will be written on pieces of paper. People will give you lots of information, in meetings, in briefings, and other teachers will pass on words of wisdom when they think of it while passing you in the corridor. Most of which you will naturally forget. Names of people you have to see, which room they're in, which deputies take care of what and dates to remember. So buy yourself a reliable notebook, this 'black book' is where all this information goes: names, numbers, even notes on classes. For example:

o You might suspect you have a SEN child in a class. Write their name down and chase it up with the SEN department.

o You might do a starter with one class that doesn't work. Make a note of it so you don't repeat the mistake.

o Note down ideas for lessons, or a teacher might give you an idea that you'd never considered.

You might think that you'll have no problem remembering all these little things, but I find even those with the best memories in a school can forget with so much going on around them.

This book should stay with you all year round, as it will always be useful.

I was once told that children are like dogs. They fight each other for a scrap, especially if it's the last bit of pizza in the canteen, smell like wet rats when they have been out in the rain (particularly Year 9 boys) and can smell fear. Not sure about the first two but the last is definitely true. At the end of the day there is only one rule – *you* are in control.

I don't think I've ever met a teacher who didn't like being in control, it's that sort of job. I would pay a teacher who could look me in the eye and say truly, 'I hated giving Johnny that detention because he called me a craggy old bitch.' Nah! You love it. There is always that line a pupil will try, 'You can't do nothin' to me'. Don't freak out – remember the truth is *they* can't do anything to *you*. You are the adult and your word will always win. Harsh? Yes. Useful? Definitely.

The best way to use this position of power is to stay calm because you always know that you are right and will win. Many teachers spend far too much energy shouting and getting worked up. Don't waste your energy. If a pupil is going to shout and yell let them, stay calm.

The key to teaching is confidence. This is not something I can give you in a book and I'm sorry about that. But I found having my own little secret helped me with my confidence. Wearing really expensive underwear or having my toenails, which were hidden in sensible black boots, bright pink gave me something to giggle to myself about when a child kicked off. You might think it would look silly smiling away to yourself but to a class of Year 8 it's confidence!

Now you might be a male teacher reading this and thinking, that's not very helpful. Who says I'm not giving you the same advice?

The first ten minutes are always the most difficult. In that time you have to get relaxed and into the swing of the class, so do a starter you are confident with and which they will find fun. It'll set you up for the full lesson. Lastly, learn to laugh at yourself. If something goes wrong it goes wrong – laugh at it and move on.

REVEALING TOO MUCH OF YOURSELF

Ask ten teachers how much you should reveal of yourself and you'll get ten different answers. There isn't a right one: sometimes it can be a good thing to give out information and at other times it isn't. Pupils will ask, mostly because they are curious. They will ask things such as your age, and whether you are married. Do you have a boyfriend? How you answer these questions may vary on the Year asking. Many people reveal more to their older students, but this can be more dangerous than admitting things to younger pupils. Remember you are their teacher, they don't want to be your friend and you shouldn't want to be theirs, so don't talk to them about the argument you had with your husband the other night, or the party you went to at the weekend – it's not important to their education. For younger pupils telling them things such as your age can finish a conversation – pupils love to think you're hiding something. They will spend a whole lesson guessing so tell them and move on. However, questions can sometimes get out of hand and they will do this because they wish to interrupt your lesson. You can simply say, 'I'm not going to talk about that now', or 'If you really want to know I'll tell you at the end of the lesson'. A pupil hasn't stayed behind yet when I've given them this option!

You must have a professional relationship with your pupils. This can be difficult in some subjects such as drama, art, PE and subjects of a more personal nature such as PSHE or citizenship. Pupils do take to some teachers; they might therefore tell you things about home or friends, and more than once you'll have someone in tears because of an argument that happened the night before.

As a teacher you are in a caring profession and you will want to be interested in their lives and put your arm around them when they come to you in floods of tears, but be careful. Schools have guidelines on physical contact and they know this; even if you put your hand on someone's back to hurry them along you could get 'Don't touch me.'

Pupils know their rights and use them often. For your first year I would make it your golden rule not to touch a pupil at all. It's not worth a misunderstanding, which can happen, so keep your distance. Teachers are also advised never to give their number or address to pupils as there is little reason for them to be calling you or sending something through the post. So don't give this information out. Allowing your pupils to have contact with you outside of school can open you up to a number of allegations. My only exception to this rule is that I give my email address to sixth formers; this does help as they can send essays even when they are on study leave and with email your postal address will not be traced by a pupil. In time you will be able to deal with this more personal side and you will learn the boundaries of different pupils. All this comes with experience.

The support system

YOUR MENTOR

I know what it was like on my training course: you never want to admit that anything is wrong and ask for help, God forbid someone might turn around and say 'I don't think teaching is really your thing.' It's stupid at training level but during your first year it's positively ridiculous. If you have a bad class or a bad pupil, or worse both, then get help. There are plenty of people available to come running and they will. The first stop is always your mentor. As a new teacher you will be given an experienced teacher to help you through the first year, and that is invaluable.

Your mentor should do the following things:

o Inform you of the school and department rules and regulations.
o Set up a period a week where they will meet you for an informal chat.
o Keep a record of these meetings for your final portfolio.
o Watch you teach, at least once a term, and write a report on it, scoring you against the government levels. You will also have a chance to write a note on this report.
o Help you to set targets and evaluate whether you have met them.
o Give you support with such things as difficult classes.

Tell your mentor of any problems that you are having with a class or pupil and they will do several things. They may want to come in to watch the class: this terrified me when my mentor proposed it but at the end of the day he wasn't there to watch *me* but to watch *them*. He made that very obvious to the class and it was nice to see they behaved just as badly with him in the room as they did when I was alone. The next thing is your mentor will probably give you a get-out clause. Take it. If you can send a pupil to another, more senior teacher when they have misbehaved then do so. This teacher should also be able to give you some good techniques for dealing with these pupils; after all they've been doing the job longer.

There are some new teachers who have problems with their mentor. This hasn't happened to me since I was training but it isn't as rare as you might think. However, if there is a problem then you must tell someone otherwise it will reflect badly on you. There will be a head of new teachers in the school and they should be someone you keep up to date with things that are happening. They will observe you and need to know if you are having any sort of problems. However you must be honest with them: some NQTs worry about admitting to problems with mentors because they think the head will side with the mentor and not with them. But you're their first concern and will appreciate your honesty. After all, tutors have responsibilities too.

THE HEAD OF NEW TEACHERS

The major problem new teachers have is that for the first half-term they still see themselves as students and therefore visitors in a school. You must quickly get it into your head that this is not the case and you will be in the school for at least a year. People make this transition in different ways – I cut all my hair off. It may have been a bit drastic as my new head of department walked straight past me on the first day. I don't know who was more embarrassed! But it made a clear distinction for me that I was no longer a student but a professional.

As far as colleagues go, I follow one rule and it has always worked for me – become friends with everyone. I do mean everyone. It is important to become friends with those in your department, they will be a constant help to you. But don't ever think that a school runs solely on the teachers: make yourself known to the office staff, the photographic person, the bursar and of course the person who looks after the whole school, the caretaker. As a teacher you will constantly be asking for favours and a friend is far more likely to say yes.

Colleagues are also a great reference as to how bad your class is – always share the worst lessons you have. I was devastated with one lesson when one of the pupils stormed out. I told a colleague about the incident and she seemed completely unaffected by it. I didn't understand this until she told me that one of her pupils had just given her a mouthful of abuse. It's good to remember it's not just your class that behaves badly.

Classroom management

RESOURCES

Sometimes the most disruptive thing a child can do is to say 'I don't have a pen'. It's simple but is a moment where potentially all hell can break loose. They can't do their work so they talk to the person next to them, then the rest of the class think it's OK to join in, and suddenly you have a classroom-management problem. Therefore, although it is a pain, *always* have spare equipment on you so when a pupil says 'I haven't got a pen' they are there on your desk and you can immediately give one to them and get them straight back on task.

Corridors can be dreadful places. Especially for new teachers. If there is a fight or pushing it is very difficult for you to discipline because the pupils don't know you and will probably ignore you, plus you don't know them so you can't jot their names down. Therefore I would always suggest you try to stay away from the corridors between lessons when it is most busy. Let the more experienced teachers handle it for now. However, do stand outside your door when waiting for your group before a class. Most schools ask you to do this anyway as it provides a presence on the corridors which prevents misbehaviour.

CORRIDORS

THE FIRST TELLING OFF

You might think that the first telling off you give is a strange part of teaching to focus a whole idea on, but as a teacher you will have to discipline many pupils and the first time is definitely the most important. Your first telling off should be in front of a whole class. Not that you should always do this – children love an audience! However if there is a child who is doing something completely inappropriate (and they will in the first couple of weeks because its great fun to wind up a new teacher), then you should tell them off there and then, making it clear to the class that you don't take any messing around. You must make sure that the telling off is justified – children hate unfairness, so be strict but fair.

Remember that the telling off you give can earn you respect from the rest of the class or lose it altogether. Think carefully about how you do it: raising your voice can be effective but don't raise it too much, try not to say just 'Don't do that' or 'No'. Give solid reasons: 'Don't push a chair away from someone as they might knock their head on it.' Then always question the pupil, 'Do you understand what I have said?' This means the pupil has to agree to the punishment and won't be able to come back with an argument.

Not being consistent is the downfall of many teachers, and not just new ones. I have already mentioned the need for fairness, and children want that more than anything else. But inconsistency can come from many sources. The least forgivable is a misunderstanding of your school's discipline policy. There is no reason for this, you must know the policies of your school inside out and follow them to the letter. You will not always agree with your school policies but you must follow them for the sake of consistency.

Inconsistency can also come from having favourites. Everyone has them – a child that they think is funny or gifted and therefore when that child steps over the line you're always a little bit soft on them. Don't be! Don't become their friend, they have friends, they have parents, play your role only and that is one of teacher.

CONSISTENCY

Why put sanctions and rewards under the same heading? Because they should be used hand in hand. Teachers find it so easy to sanction, but rewards are 100 times more effective than sanctions. Roughly, you should give five rewards for every sanction. Particularly try to reward those who usually end up with more sanctions. However, a warning – rewards can undo sanctions. Don't give a sanction for them shouting out then give five rewards for them answering one question properly – you're undermining yourself.

Rewards and sanctions can also fall into the area of inconsistency. It's easy to give children whom you wish to encourage rewards for just sitting in their chair for more then three minutes, but it will be unpopular.

Your school will have rewards merits or stamps, so use them. You can also add your own rewards, e.g. computer time, a film or a game at the end of the lesson. These are obviously for whole classes and work well as it gets pupils to control each other: you'll get 'shut up Tom or we won't get to play a game' and they calm down far more quickly.

Many teachers give out sweets but I always worry about the health issue, so give out silly-shaped rubbers or have them bring in a song they like and for the person who has worked the best let them play their choice of song at the end. All this helps towards a productive classroom.

Children have this game they love playing. It's called 'how to freak out a teacher'. They do it with new teachers, student teachers and their favourite, supply teachers. They will test you. To help yourself you should make your boundaries as clear as possible right from the beginning; however, think carefully about what you want those boundaries to be. No teacher wants a classroom of silent pupils. You want them to be aware that their opinions are important but at the same time they must have respect for both you and others in the class. You should not have different boundaries for each. There should be silence for instance when the teacher is speaking, just as there should be when a pupil is speaking. And that includes from the teacher – don't talk over pupils, give them the respect you expect.

Ensure you don't just say that a rule is a rule without explaining why or how it will be beneficial to the students, because they have little interest in how it will be beneficial to you. Some teachers find it a good idea to have pupils write these boundaries in their books. This makes for a constant visual reminder.

Make it clear what you will take and what you won't and don't be unrealistic. For example it isn't realistic for children working in groups to be silent. But asking them to ensure they only talk in their groups and not across the classroom to other people *is* realistic. Give them the reason for this, otherwise you will constantly be asked why.

SETTING THE BOUNDARIES

So many of the teachers I meet have a strict layout: pupils sit in rows, or a horse shoe, and often they are boy/girl or are in alphabetical order. I prefer a little trust. Let them sit where they want on the understanding that it is a privilege, and one they can lose if they take advantage. This way you have already, without any knowledge of them, shown trust in them and they appreciate this. As for the right layout, every teacher is different, but one rule that should be made is that no pupil should have to turn around to see you, they should always be facing you and you should be able to reach every child quickly and easily.

YOUR CLASSROOM LAYOUT

Your five golden rules of behaviour management should be:

1 Listen to experience and advice – many teachers can be snobby about taking on other people's strategies. Don't be, we're all in the same boat.

2 Make your head of department or mentor aware of behaviour problems in the classroom – so many teachers, particularly new ones, don't like to admit there is a problem. People will judge you if you keep silent so don't.

3 Don't be afraid to do something totally different – shock your pupils. Many teachers who have issues in the classroom end up doing something really safe such as writing because you think well, at least you can control them in that activity. This is wrong! Instead have them do something really special: take them out on the field to do nature poems or Greek theatre, have them doing videos or photos for science or history, just because they are 'bad' kids doesn't mean they don't deserve an interesting education!

4 Get the behaviour into perspective – how bad are they really? Are they just chatty or do they physically hurt each other? Because unless it's the latter you don't have a huge problem.

5 Use the school system – you are not alone in having to deal with bad behaviour in the classroom, although it can sometimes feel like that.

FIVE GOLDEN RULES OF BEHAVIOUR MANAGEMENT

PERSONAL SAFETY

Personal safety is another one of the issues that you would have talked a lot about during your training but it may have seemed less important then, as you would always have had another teacher with you – which is obviously not the case in a normal school. Therefore always be aware of what is going on around you.

○ If you are telling a pupil off privately after class then ensure you are standing where you can get to the door.

○ Always have room between you and the pupil, you should never invade their space anyway but when you are alone with them you need to have space in case they attack you.

○ Also be aware that in some cases pupils will get violent. Some of these pupils would have been 'flagged up' and if a pupil is known for violent behaviour then don't discipline them when you are by yourself.

○ Don't try to stop a pupil leaving a room if they are in a violent mood. It is not worth ever putting yourself at risk.

○ You can pass the matter on to senior management and let them discipline the pupil later. Don't put yourself in a situation you can't get out of.

Child protection is something they would have talked about in lectures. You will have read all the documents on it and you may even have written a long essay on it. That's the theory, the practice is far more difficult.

As a teacher you are in a position where you see pupils every day, you notice their changes in mood and you notice how they turn out in the morning, are they clean, clothed properly, etc.?

You will also be in a position to hear things that are said, sometimes by the student, sometimes about a student. Listen to these, 90 per cent of the time it might be silly gossip but sometimes you will hear things that need to be acted upon. For example, if you hear that Sally is being sick all the time she is in school this is something that needs to be checked out.

If you hear anything or see something, or you are just worried, you need to take action. It is better to waste time checking something that turns out to be nothing than leave a child who might need your help. The first person to go to is their tutor, they will know the pupil. Tell them what your concerns are, are they aware of this, is there an explanation? Mostly there will be, but if not they will be glad to have the information. From here they may talk to the pupil and if it is serious they can inform the head of year/house and pastoral head. You should check with the tutor how this is going. You may be asked to talk to the head of house so they get the information right. After this keep track of what's going on, particularly if you teach the pupil. Remember, any information about a pupil is private. Do not discuss it with other staff or with other pupils.

CHILD PROTECTION

You will often find that in 'bad' groups there is a ring-leader, the one that sets them all off. Often the other pupils will know who it is but it might take you a bit longer to work it out. Once you have found this child take them away from the rest of the class and say, 'I think you are the reason for the bad behaviour in my class, do you agree?' If they say no then tell them that you are going to focus on their behaviour and highlight it to them after the class.

You will often find that this child loves being told off in front of a class as this gives them the attention they crave, so wait until after the class.

However, to understand a badly behaved child you must also look elsewhere; look at the family life – are they not encouraged at home? Do they have a violent home life? If so you need to know this and it will help you in how to deal with them.

Lastly, they are not just your responsibility. Tell the head of department, ring the parents; always ensure that the school is dealing with the pupil, not just you. You are there to teach, not to be a zookeeper.

Everyone has a class they dread, the class that brings them to the brink of quitting. And it's not just new teachers – those who have been teaching for 20 years still have dreadful classes. The first thing to remember when dealing with this kind of group is that everyone has been or is in the same position. Sharing this fact is important so talk to other teachers, particularly other new teachers. This will help you realize that the group's behaviour has little thing to do with you and your teaching but is being little buggers, plain and simple.

of books on classroom management:
Behave 2 (Continuum) by Sue
ourites. Bill Rogers' *Cracking the*
anaging the Harder than
pman Publishing) is both useful
ese books will give you plenty of

st of ideas that are really worth trying:

e the seating.

nge the work. I even changed an entire scheme of work for one of my bad groups (yes I had more than one).

○ Keep lessons active, short tasks as opposed to long ones.

○ Treat them once in a while. Maybe to end every good lesson they'll see ten minutes of a film, or play a game. Reward good behaviour as well as punishing bad.

○ But most of all don't lose it, stay calm with them – classes love it when a teacher screams and shouts. If they get louder you should simply get quieter. Lowering your voice will eventually force them to do the same.

However, as hard as you try sometimes things just don't get any better. If this happens, it doesn't mean you are a bad teacher, the best thing to do is to get some proper support.

INVOLVING PUPILS

Remember that bad behaviour is down to the pupils: it is their decision to talk when you are or get out of their seats when they shouldn't. Therefore involve them in making rules for the classroom, particularly if your school doesn't have a very detailed discipline programme. Talk to the class about the problems they are having. You may even want to do this on a one-to-one basis.

Go back to basics and also remember not to have lots of rules as these will be difficult to enforce. It's best to start with five basic rules such as 'No talking when the teacher or another pupil is speaking'. You can then build on these as other more specific problems arise.

For younger pupils or small SEN groups you could make up an actual contract for them to write their rules on and sign. You, of course, should also sign this and perhaps some of the rules might be especially for you, for example one of them could be 'Miss/Sir will always write the homework on the board'. It's good for the pupils to understand that while there are expectations of them there are expectations of you too. Make sure you have these rules up somewhere clearly on display and that you use them consistently.

I am a young woman with no children. You might not think that is a strange thing but I have found that as a teacher parents can use it against you. There have been a number of times when talking to parents that they have said, 'Have you got children?' I am always disheartened by this because I do not believe that I am a less effective teacher just because I don't have any children of my own. However, it did make me think about how we don't deal just with children but also with their parents. Some of whom can be just as difficult as (if not more difficult than) the child.

While learning about and researching young people you should also therefore research parenting: it is important to know where they are coming from, what they are having to deal with and how they deal with it, if they do at all. The BBC produces wonderful programmes such as *Little Angels* and the new show *Teen Angels*. However, Channel 4's *Super Nanny*, which shows how children display bad behaviour in the home with advice on how to handle it, can also give you an insight into what some parents see as behaviour management.

When faced with a totally horrid class you must deal with it as quickly as possible. Don't allow yourself to get more and more depressed about it. One bad group can ruin your first year of teaching if you let them. They can make it difficult for you to do a good job because as soon as you walk in you're on edge, and the pupils will notice it. It's very easy in your first year to feel isolated, it's you 'against' 30 pupils and there can often be a lack of support in the classroom.

It doesn't have to be this way. The first rule here is to understand that they are not just *your* responsibility. Remember at the end of the day you are a teacher not a zookeeper – you are not paid enough to deal with their rubbish, and trust me they have plenty to dish out. There are those in the school, heads of department, house or faculty, who are paid a lot more than you and certainly have more experience: bad groups are their responsibility, so pass the buck. Shout 'help' and shout it loud.

Every school is full of people who are experienced in education and who can help you, particularly when you're new and having difficulties. Here is a list of people you should go to:

○ Your mentor and the head of new teachers are always good ports of call for general bad behaviour in the classroom, especially if you feel you are starting to lose control over the pupils.

○ If you have problems with certain individuals, such as a pupil who is rarely in your class and when they do turn up they are so far behind they just cause havoc, then the person you need to talk to is their form tutor. They will know the pupil on a more personal level and may be able to give you some insight into the situation.

○ If this doesn't give you the information you need, talk to the head of year/house or the head of pastoral care as they will have an overview of the entire situation including other family members who may attend the same school. There may be an issue at home, or home might need to be made aware of the problems.

○ Some pupils might seem to have behaviour issues when really it's a special needs issue. Check the special needs register: do they have dyslexia or Irene syndrome? If so you might need to ask the SEN department how to handle it – does the pupil need worksheets on a special coloured paper, for instance? Or maybe they need extra support and you need to see if a Learning Support Assistant could come in for that lesson.

If you have nowhere else to go then speak to the pupil and ask him/her what's going on.

NEVER LET THEM SEE YOU CRY

Being on the verge of tears can happen to most teachers at some point. It could be because of a class or a particular pupil, or it could be that you are just over-tired and over-worked and suddenly can't take the little thing that you would have been fine with any other day of the week.

It happens to us all I'm sure. The important thing is not to let your pupils see it. Although this can be very hard, it's even harder to come back from breaking down in front of a class. The one time I cried in class I was lucky they were leaving for the day and this allowed me to run into the English office and hide. The first thing one of the teachers in there said to me was 'Did any of them see you?' *Never* let them see you upset, they don't deserve the satisfaction. So whatever you have to do in front of the pupils keep a solid face and, if you must let it all out, do so after the class has left.

The new kid on the block

Remember you are not a teacher until you pass your first year. To check your suitability as a teacher you will be observed throughout the year by your head of department, head of new teachers and possibly others such as head of faculty.

Too many people don't take this seriously. You would never have imagined going to an observed lesson at university without:

○ a well-planned lesson that met the needs of all learners (auditory, kinaesthetic and visual)
○ a copy of the plan for the observer
○ your resources especially designed with differentiation and extension tasks.

Therefore don't ever imagine having an observed lesson without these in your first year of teaching. I am very aware that as a teacher you would find this impossible to do for every lesson but it's about giving your observer what they expect, so play their game.

If possible pick classes that you know are interesting in slots where you have a 'free' before hand so you can be there really early and set up – after lunch or break is a good idea.

Remember this is what decides whether or not you are going to be a teacher so put everything you have into it.

Most students get an inadequate observation at some point while training. You either get this in your training year or your first year of teaching. But getting it in your first year of teaching is most upsetting. This can make new teachers very demoralized. What you have to ensure is that it doesn't push you over the edge.

Talk to your mentor: was it just a bad day? Or were you ill? If there is a genuine reason for you under-performing most mentors will overlook it. If they are realistic they will throw it in the bin and give you another chance. Be grateful. If this happens you will need to be observed again sooner rather than later.

One of the hardest things is to be honest with yourself. Listen carefully to the criticism and ask yourself:

○ Is it fair?
○ Was your behaviour management just not up to scratch?
○ Did you pitch the level too high or too low?
○ Was the lesson just plain boring?

It's only when you admit this that you can improve; if you keep saying to yourself 'I think that was a great lesson' you'll never move on.

Take the advice of your mentor and keep it in mind when planning your next lesson. Ask another teacher to have a look at it and see if it's all right – maybe they can offer you some suggestions. Then forget about the observation that went wrong and go and prove that this is the profession you want to be in.

THAT BAD OBSERVATION

As a new teacher you will want to make your mark on a school. This is a great idea. Don't forget teaching is only one part of the profession, there are many other things to do in a school. Making your mark will give you something fun to do and will allow you to get to know the pupils on a different level. You will also need to do this for your personal development.

There are many things you can do to make your mark in a school: arrange trips, special classes and clubs. This is great but stay within your limits and be realistic about what those limits are – you're a new teacher, the learning curve is steep and falling off will give you a very bruised bottom.

Don't try foreign trips – too much can go wrong and the stress is not worth it. Plus new teachers will not usually be given permission to run an overnight trip, so even if you are staying in this country, get the pupils home for the night. It is a good idea to volunteer for other teachers' overnight trips, though, in the hope that you can learn what to do without taking all the risks.

It is not a good idea to take pupils out during the school day. Many schools are testy about this now and it's not a great way to start off your teaching career. Instead, do the evenings: a 7.30pm theatre performance, or a Saturday. Trips are great but focus on your paperwork: there will be a risk assessment to do, letters to write and get signed, coaches and tickets to organize, health forms to collect and money to get in. Something pupils are never good at. But don't get me wrong – it is worth it.

For your own benefit come up with certain rules and keep to them. Firstly be flexible, if it's a club then make it clear that you might have to cancel it at the last minute; this gives you a get-out clause. Secondly make sure that you wrap up clubs and societies way before the end of term, about four weeks before the summer. Trust me, you won't feel like being enthusiastic and happy when you have Year 11 coursework to mark, A-levels to worry about and your summer holiday to organize!

The first thing I did on my own was to organize a Christmas Show. I was terrified: I thought the pupils would forget their lines, no one would come, we'd lose money and it would be a complete disaster. I hoped for 50 people, 250 came and our hall only holds 200 (well it did before that night)!

USE YOUR YOUTH

Pupils do seem to find it easier to relate to a young teacher and therefore it is wise to play on this. Have energy, talk their language more. Many teachers, sometimes without knowing, use language that is inappropriate. They might say 'That's good work' but saying it's 'wicked' is often more of a compliment. Also take note of what they like: children go through phases, one minute it's *Little Britain*, the next *Harry Potter* and then scoobies (these are the annoying plastic bracelets they make under the table while you're teaching). The point is that often you can use these fads to your advantage. I had a difficult class and I was teaching grammar, several of the class were boys and I knew they read and enjoyed the Harry Potter books so I read them (yes all of them) and used them in the class as examples. Or you might want to set up a competition; e.g. the one to do the best essay will get a scoobie.

Everyone can remember their schooldays. Think really hard about them and ask friends you were at school with, to get a different viewpoint.

Remember the teachers you liked and disliked and think about the reasons why, what was it about them? Maybe they made you feel small and unimportant, maybe it didn't matter how often you put your hand up they would never ask you, or they'd leave you to the last which meant someone would have stolen your idea. Learn from their mistakes but at the same time learn and copy what they did right. If it worked for them it can work for you. Maybe you fondly remember a teacher because they always dressed in bright clothes or because no matter how busy they were they always said hello. Thinking back to your schooldays makes you see school from the pupils' point of view.

REMEMBER YOUR SCHOOLDAYS

It is very easy when you are a new teacher to be taken advantage of. The teachers who do it probably don't mean to ask too much of you, to them you going on a trip to the theatre because someone has dropped out at the last minute might not seem like a cliff to climb, but if you had put that time away to do a lesson plan then you are in danger of compromising the quality of your lesson (and perhaps your health). Remember everything takes you longer and therefore your time is precious. Of course one of the biggest problems is that as a new teacher you want to be seen to be helpful, interested in extra-curricular activities (see Making your mark, p. 54) and most importantly supporting other staff members when they're in a scrape – all of this you should do, but it can come at a price.

The worst thing is if it's a head of department or faculty who's asking you. You know these people are important and will be making the decision about whether or not you pass at the end of the year but you must learn that they will respect you just as much if you say 'I'm sorry I can't tonight, but put me down as a definite next time and I will ask around to see if anyone else can help out.' Remember – be realistic about your time and be careful of going beyond the call of duty too much.

As has often been said teaching is about being confident, not just in front of a class but in your own ability. After all, you've got this far. Remember you are newly trained, everything you know is brand new and up to date, and because of that try not to be influenced too much by others who have been in the profession for many, many years. They might use classroom management techniques from the 1940s but strategies on teaching and particularly classroom management change all the time, there is always a new practitioner publishing books, or new government strategies and you will know all the modern buzz words.

You can use the experience of other teachers of course, they will know the students better and maybe have strategies that work with certain ones. They have been around and will advise you but don't just take their advice straight off. Think about what you know and what you have tried and don't be put off. It's your career, and you will have to try out some of the things you've learnt at some point.

JUST BECAUSE YOU'RE NEW DOESN'T MEAN YOU'RE WRONG

BE OUTRAGEOUS

New teachers come to the profession with big ideas, lots of energy and the belief that the job is important and worthy. Remind yourself of this every time a pupil swears at you or when you come home saying you'll never go back.

You'll have more energy now at the beginning of your career than at any other time so do something which reflects that, use interesting and unusual stimuli, be outrageous – if you are doing the Battle of Hastings then recreate it on the field. Don't be scared to do something a bit different just because others do 'normal' lessons. It can be scary, you might have a bad class and not know whether or not you should try your wacky idea, just remember you have nothing to lose and everything to gain so try new things and always remember you are doing a really important job.

The reality of being a teacher

MEETINGS

You will have:

o Faculty meetings
o Departmental meetings
o Staff meetings
o SEN meetings
o Gifted and talented meetings
o New-staff meetings.

And this is just the basics. As a new teacher you need to be everywhere all the time – the most difficult thing is *remembering* to go to them all as well as finding the time to go. By my second term the head of new teachers had pretty much given up any hope of ever seeing me at one of her meetings. There was always something, 'I have a rehearsal', 'I have a theatre trip', 'I have to spend two hours looking for an extra set of wings because Peter Pan thought it was funny to pull off Tinkerbell's wings'.

You get the basic idea! But I got the information anyway and that's the important thing. How? It's called buying your fellow first-year teachers a drink and borrowing their notes. Even my head of department took to giving me an agenda with a note at the bottom saying 'Will understand if you can't attend'. I would love to imagine that all heads of departments are this understanding but I'm afraid it isn't the case.

Meetings should be on your school calendar right at the beginning of the year so try to plan other activities at a different time. Also put down when your meetings are so you don't double- or triple-book yourself. Whenever someone asks you to attend a meeting check before saying yes. No one will mind you saying 'I'll check my diary and tell you tomorrow'.

But when you do make it to the odd meeting make sure you use it to your full advantage. It might be terrifying but make sure you voice your opinions. You are no longer a student, you are paid to work at your school. You want the school to be the best for your pupils and for yourself, so speak up because everyone has an opinion.

Reports are the bane of every teacher's life. Take a look at your timetable: if you have four Year 7 groups you can tell in advance when you will be at your busiest. So plan for this. The biggest problem I have, and I admit it wholeheartedly, is that I rarely remember all the pupils I teach. Well you don't do you, you remember those that get into trouble because yelling their name across a class can prevent them from throwing a punch, you remember the really nice ones because they answer all your questions, and you can sometimes forget the others. Not to mention the fact that parents seem to go through phases of names. I have several Roberts in one class. Some of them I only see once a week, some of them I only see for half the year, you may be in the same position. Make notes on your classes during the year so when you come to your reports you have notes on each of the pupils. It sounds like more paperwork but, trust me, it saves time just when you don't have enough to go around.

There are also some 'cheats' that can be used, and more teachers use them than you might think – even if they don't admit it. Write a summary of what the pupils have been doing. Parents want to know and you can use 50 words to tell them – put it at the beginning of every report.

Prepare, in advance, typical phrases you will use, 'Robert must work harder if he is to reach his true potential', 'Robert needs to focus more on his classwork as opposed to talking to his friends', 'Robert is a hardworking student and a pleasure to teach'. You'll do this naturally so it's quicker to do it in advance and cut and paste. Some faculties have a sentence bank they all use with phrases that come up time and time again – you may want to see if this is the case in your school.

Remember, every pupil should have at least two targets – put these as bullet points as it uses up space.

Time is one of the worst enemies for a teacher –
sometimes you don't have enough and sometimes you
have too much, particularly when you are in class.
Getting the timing of your lesson right is really
important, particularly for a new teacher. If you dismiss a
class late then you are cutting down on your time to get
to your next class, which any new teacher knows could
be anywhere in the school, and/or you cut down on the
amount of preparation time you have for your next class.

However you don't want to be tied to your watch. It is
terrible when you are talking to pupils to keep looking at
your watch – they will think you're not paying attention
to them. Instead have a clock on the desk that you can
take everywhere with you, and make it a digital one. This
clock should be set to the school's time. Yes, schools
have a habit of being in a totally different time zone to
everywhere else so check the time on the first bell and
stick with it.

Also plan in time for things like commuting: your
pupils might have had a lesson on the other side of the
school and it will take them 5 minutes to get to you.

I find the worst thing is having spare time at the end,
when you have finished all your planned work. If pupils
are hanging around waiting for the bell they are talking,
they are fighting, and they will go to their next class like
this. So have a game up your sleeve that is timeless.
Drama and PE are easy, but even in something like
geography play hangman with the technical terms that
they have learnt that lesson.

New teachers are protected as far as timetables go.
You will have a reduced timetable and you will need it
because things will take you longer than they do anyone
else. You should also have protected free periods, which
means you shouldn't be put on cover. However this can
happen – once or twice might be acceptable but mention
any more to your mentor. You need your free periods, so
take them.

The biggest danger new teachers have with these free
periods is that you end up relying on them. You think 'I
won't do that photocopying because I can do it in period
one' but I guarantee that as soon as you fall into that
trap something will happen: a pupil will need seeing, or
an important memo will have to be answered, and
suddenly you're off to class with no resources.

Free periods are a blessing but don't get too casual
about them. Also, very importantly, don't waste them: it
is time that you have outside the classroom so do some
marking, or photocopying for the following week. Time
well spent here is time you won't have to spend
elsewhere, like after school!

TIMETABLE

Marking. It's time-consuming and it's boring. But there are ways around it, not all of which you should admit to doing, so don't read this chapter in the staffroom – leave now!

If possible timetable marking into your working week. New teachers have to be given a certain number of free periods, so take advantage of them and put on your time-table which books you'll mark when. Then stick to it.

There are other little tricks. Have pupils mark each other's work. English teachers can play 'Let's work on our dictionary skills. I want you all to check your own spellings.' Maths and science teachers can simply say 'Mark your partner's work while I read out the answers.' All subjects have a way of getting the pupils to self-mark. You might say this is cheating – well, you obviously have more time than I do. No, to be serious – this sort of exercise will do them good; the government is very keen on having pupils play an active role in their learning and this does exactly that.

The worst part of marking is levelling or grading work. If work is being levelled then you do need to read it in great detail, so you should set aside a block of time. It is far easier if you do this, particularly when you are still unsure about your class and the levelling system of the school to get into a flow. You get to the point where Sally must be a level 5 because she mentioned things Max did and he was a level 5. The examples are nice and fresh in your head and your marking will go a lot faster. The worst thing is marking long essays that are on the same subject – five essays on William Blake and you feel like drowning yourself!

My first group of essays took 25 minutes each and there were 35 in the class! A teacher on my PGCE placement sat me down and told me to watch and time him marking an A-level essay. I did so. He did it in 8 minutes flat. I was stunned. The secret? Well firstly you can't beat experience, but secondly he didn't waste time on things like comments. Instead for good things he'd give one tick, for very good things he'd give two ticks and where a comment *was* needed he would write a symbol or letter and assured me that the pupils knew what they meant. I've tried it and no, I can't do it in 8 minutes, but it doesn't take me 25 minutes any more either!

ICT CAN BE YOUR WORST ENEMY

In today's society more and more businesses and services are using ICT to do all the paperwork and schools are no different. It is very likely that if your school isn't already using a computer program to do reports and things such as that, it soon will be. The problem is computers are just not reliable. The worst thing is seeing a teacher who has spent their only free period of the week writing reports only to have them suddenly and for no reason at all disappear. You can't afford to lose this time so, although this may sound really over the top, save everything, every few sentences and a number of times. It is always better to have two back-ups than one. Plus be careful if your school gives you disks, it's most likely they will be very old and inclined to wipe themselves, so spend the money and buy your own.

Parents' evenings can be one of the most terrifying things in your first year. It's bad enough being in front of children but being in front of parents is even worse. Not to mention that some parents are rather pushy. Friends at school teased me about how parents come with lawyers and notepads, and they weren't far off – there are always some parents who take notes! The best thing to do is to watch the classes whose parents you're going to meet a couple of weeks before so you have up-to-date information on them, and take along their exercise books: this is particularly helpful when you don't know which child goes with which parent.

The worst-case scenario of course is the irate parent. These parents have no interest in listening to you and aren't really interested in their child's progression – they just want to argue, and you're just there at the wrong time. In this case you need to keep the parent calm; don't make any promises and don't make up excuses. Ask them if they wish to make an appointment with you at a later date for a longer meeting or with a senior member of staff or the head of department. Senior management are more experienced at dealing with parents and asking parents to see senior members of staff will also make them think that you are taking this issue seriously rather than doing what you are doing and passing them on.

PARENTS EVENINGS

YOUR BAG

Most new teachers don't have a classroom, which means you are forever in different areas of the school. This of course means you have to carry everything around with you, so as far as your bag goes get one with wheels.

However, because this bag will go everywhere with you take note of what you have in it. Any confidential papers shouldn't be carried around; you never know where you might leave them.

You should always carry with you:

o Your timetable. It's easy to get lessons or rooms mixed up so don't take the chance.

o Your register.

o Your lesson plans.

o I also carry an emergency activity to do. It's very easy when you don't have a classroom to get to a room and remember you have left the class books or the resources somewhere else. You can send a pupil for them but you need something for the class to do for those ten minutes – a starter suitable for all classes, for instance.

o A bottle of water – it keeps your voice healthy.

o A snack. In case you can't get to the staffroom at break before all the flapjacks have gone.

Some new teachers are lucky enough to have their own desk, but even if you don't in your first year you will eventually. This desk will always be in view of pupils and other members of staff and should therefore be tidy.

I have a tower of trays to keep folders in, folder holders to keep papers in, pen holders and notelets so students can leave me messages. But most importantly I don't leave at the end of the day until I have cleared and tidied my desk. Why? If pupils – particularly the older ones – see a mess and papers all over the place they will assume you are disorganized and may even lose their work.

YOUR CLASSROOM

Like your desk, you might not get this in your first year but you can hope! Your classroom should also be tidy, and make sure you have bright displays, some with pupils' work on it. You should also display the school rules and your own, especially if you teach subjects such as drama or science that have rules for safety. Have these displayed prominently and simply.

There are also a number of places where you can get educational posters. You can, for example try publishing houses: HarperCollins produces a lot of educational books and will provide you with posters; see their website, www.fireandwater.com. Schofield and Sims, www.schofieldandsims.co.uk, specialize in publishing educational books and do a number of subject-specific posters. If you want more general posters about education and life after school see Jaguar Educational UK Ltd, www.jaguared.co.uk, which produces these and has a catalogue you can send away for. It's also worth asking your head of faculty about posters, as companies often send them through the post.

I also had a 'Ha ha' wall which simply had jokes and funny poems on it. There are lots of lovely books that are easy to get hold of on www.amazon.co.uk such as *Excuses, excuses: Poems about school* by John Foster (Oxford University Press). So try to make your displays fun as well as academic.

As a new teacher you need to be aware that schools are full of gossip. You will find out very quickly, if you listen carefully, that teachers group themselves: they will have their 'friends' and their 'enemies', they will gossip about people. The best thing for you to do as a new teacher is to stay out of it. Yes you want to make friends and you want to know what's going on but like all gossip it can get out of hand, and the last thing you need in your first year is to be mixed up in gossip and arguments. Stay on everyone's side and if people ask your opinion about someone stay neutral. If the worst comes to the worst say you don't know them because you're new and walk away.

Don't forget that some people might have a reputation for being miserable or unhelpful, but if this is the case try some advice my mother gave me. Talk to them, find out what they like and meet them halfway. You would be surprised at how a little thing like talking to someone about what they like can bring them out of a hardened shell.

STAFFROOM GOSSIP

Even as a new teacher there will be things that must be done to a deadline and not all of these will be big things such as reports. Reports, etc. are easy to remember to do because they play a big part in the school year but you will have smaller jobs to do that are just as important. For instance you will get SEN memos on pupils where you might have to write a short paragraph on how they are getting on. Or it might be for supervision for the school disco and you need to tick the time you can do and give it back to the organizer. Little things like this are so easy to forget but can cause you real problems, not to mention make you look disorganized. The best thing is to do them as soon as you get them: if it's a tick and a signature then do it there and then and hand it in.

If you have some that need to be thought about, collect them and set aside a period in the week to do it but take note of the deadline, for little jobs like this you might only have a couple of days.

Most schools will have end-of-year tests for all years, but as a new teacher it is likely that you will get a group which will end the year with some very important exams such as Year 9 or sixth form. It is unlikely you will get a Year 11 group, but not unheard of. If this is the case you need to focus on these groups, just being a new teacher doesn't excuse anything going wrong.

You should:

○ Plan your lessons well in advance and show them to your head of department.

○ Talk to other teachers doing the same years and ask them what they do, how they do it and, most importantly, the timing.

○ Ensure you start coursework at the right time, do enough pieces and complete it within the time given.

○ Get hold of the exam spec, read it all and make sure you check with someone if there is *anything* you don't understand.

EXAM PRESSURE

A BIT WACKY

I know teachers, male and female, who come in every day with a dark suit on, white shirt and shiny shoes. Look at it from a pupil's point of view: yes you must look respectable and neat and like a teacher, but it must be boring looking at a dark suit all day. Therefore try to have a wacky item that just makes things a bit more individual and interesting.

There are a number of fabulous ties around, particularly at Christmas at Marks & Spencer and any tie shop such as Tie Rack. Get one with animals on or cartoon characters. I know a teacher who has one with dinosaurs on and he's a history teacher!

Female teachers have it harder to some degree, but I have a pair of earrings that are the comedy and tragedy faces. Wearing nice jewellery can often do the trick – it's just something a bit more interesting. This can of course help in class. If you are pointing to something on the board, wear a nice ring: they'll focus on it and therefore focus on the board!

I have a bad memory. I know I do and as a teacher there is a lot to remember, small and big. A good idea is to leave messages for yourself in places where you know you will see them.

If people have asked me to bring something in or I need a book or video I ring home and leave a message for myself on the answerphone. This way either I go home, see the message light blinking, listen to the message and immediately put what I need in my bag, or my housemate comes home, listens to it and reminds me. Either way I don't forget.

Also leave messages on doors that you know you look at. I have a sweetie cupboard that I visit at least five times a day (I have a sweet tooth!), stick labels on here where you will see them. The other great place is on the toilet door (as long as your toilet faces one of course). Well, at least it gives you something to read.

At some point during the first week of school you will be asked (well, told) to do a break-time duty. Remember, they can't make you do lunchtime duty but break-time ones are different. There are two definitions of a break-time duty. The first is the one the school will give you. 'Teachers will, for the duration of the school break, gently parade around small designated areas keeping a watchful eye over pupils during their recreational period.' The other definition is the one the teachers will give you and that is 'Break duty is 20 minutes of hell.' Walking through wind and rain and dodging snowballs. You spend the whole time chancing upon smokers, never actually finding out who the culprits are because they either lie through their braces or run away and you of course, being new to the school, have no idea what their names are. You'll break up several fights, probably in the first week, and you'll always be late to the class you have afterwards.

However this is a punishment all teachers must face and therefore here are a few handy tips to get you through:

○ Always prepare for the worst weather. I guarantee it will pour down when the only thing you have on is a white shirt!

○ Take something to do. No, not marking, it's too messy in the rain. I mean something to eat; I always find it useful when I'm ignoring pupils to have a packet of food to bury my head in. Well, it's your break too.

○ Try to walk around with another member of staff. Back-up is always important.

○ When all else fails, when it's pouring with rain and the wind is howling like something in the drama studio, get talking to your head of department – they'll keep you for the full 20 minutes.

Undertaking bus duty can seem like a simple thing but the details are important. Your school will have buses that come to collect pupils at the end of the day. This is different from the morning because after school they will all come at the same time and you could have hundreds of pupils and around half a dozen buses.

Staff have to do bus duty for safety reasons but this in itself is the snag because you have to ensure that you are just as safe.

If you are asked to do a bus duty talk to your mentor. It is unusual for new teachers to have to do a duty like this but it may be there is no other choice for the school. If you have to do it, check whether or not a member of senior staff will be there, because if so it will be they that take the responsibility, not you, and this is a responsibility that you don't want at this stage in your career. If senior management are not there and you are expected to do it with maybe another new teacher voice your concerns. Also check if they have certain gear for you to wear. You should, particularly in winter, be given a high-visibility coat so you can be seen in the dark. If this isn't the case stay somewhere safe, either away from the buses altogether or stand on the first step of the bus to see the pupils on.

BUS DUTY

THE PAY CHEQUE

New teachers are often in a difficult position when it comes to money. They will often have debts from their original degree, which serve as a constant nagging at the back of the head. You will most likely have an overdraft that seemed like a good idea at the time, and usually a frightening amount of money on your credit cards, which slowly gains interest. (If you don't have the latter, by the way, you will by Christmas.)

Of course, the major problem most NQTs have is that it's the first time in four years they have had money and a little craziness slips in. I bought a Gucci watch. But even with all this extra money and banks offering you money (which they do when you let slip your profession), new teachers are often left short. There are ways round this but every school has its own rules, so check with someone who knows before you go and get yourself into trouble. The best way of making a little extra money is to tutor. Yes, I realize that the thought of teaching pupils outside school hours as well as inside school hours seems like a ghastly way to spend what little free time you have, but it really isn't that bad. Don't forget pupils who get tutors often want to do well and they behave well because their parents are paying for it (and rarely let them forget that).

Lunchtime duty is another way to get a little extra cash. It doesn't pay much but money is money! You should read the section on duties beforehand and think about how much you really need the extra cash. Finally, the most important thing to remember when it comes to your money (and let's be honest it's why we take the jobs that we do) is that the wage slip comes every month and you get a pay rise twice a year. Bliss!

It is no secret that for most teachers Wednesday is the worst day of the week. You have already been working for two days and you are still two days away from the weekend. This does seem to make a difference, so more importantly than ever get to bed early on a Tuesday, and if you can treat yourself on a Wednesday night do so. Having a mid-week treat is a really good idea: it breaks the week up for you, because it's easy to think you should just work solidly for 5 days, but going out on a Wednesday night gives you a break where you need it the most.

But be careful what you do on a Wednesday night. You still have two days of teaching left and they will seem ever so long if you are overtired.

MID-WEEK DESPAIR

FRIDAYS ARE SACRED

The worst idea I ever had was to have a drama club on a Friday after school.

You can imagine: all your classes have been noisy and busy and all you want to do is crawl home, sit in front of the TV and watch a good movie. Instead you have to be enthusiastic and creative for fifteen Year 8 and 9 pupils who are blowing off all their energy that's been piling up during the week. So take it from someone who has already made that mistake – never book anything on a Friday. Friday is one of only two days that you can stay out late and have a lie in the next day, so go out and enjoy yourself.

If you are very lucky your Sunday blues won't set in until after Christmas. Everyone knows the basic feeling – it gets to about 2 o'clock on Sunday and you start to go through the classes you have the next day. You remember that you have your sixth-form class and wonder if any of them will make it out of bed in time for the 9 o'clock lesson. You realize you have your terrible Year 7, who are always hyperactive on a Monday because you have them after lunch, and lastly it dawns on you that you have a meeting after school which will probably go on until 5 and will make you miss *Escape to the Country* (which you'd never admit to watching).

Suddenly a weight of depression passes over you and lands firmly on your head, giving you a headache for the rest of the day and no energy to do anything but sit in front of the TV mulling over the bad day you're going to have. Don't do it! Sunday is one of only two days that you get off a week – don't waste it thinking about something you can't stop.

One way or another Monday morning will come and one way or another your sixth form will or will not turn up, regardless of how long you think about it. Instead, put your energy into enjoying your last day of freedom. Regardless of how you have decided to handle your weekend, spend the afternoon/evening doing something you want to do. But don't sit at home – you'll only think about work. Go out somewhere, have a walk, go shopping, go for a drink, go to the cinema or the theatre.

However, a warning: there is a limit. Don't stay out till three in the morning drinking: this will *not* help. Monday morning is bad enough without adding a hangover or tiredness to it, so get to bed well before the sun comes up.

SUNDAY BLUES

My friends get very jealous of me. I get a week at half-term – twice a year. Two weeks' holiday at Christmas, two weeks at Easter and, to add further insult, six weeks during the summer. But there is a catch that few people, particularly the pupils, know about. Most teachers actually spend their holidays working! Be it collecting resources, planning lessons or marking, there always seems to be something that needs to be done. The key to success is to get a balance. The balance that will suit you might not be the same for everyone else so you must find out what works for you. This will depend on other aspects of your life. If your partner is a teacher it's far easier as you will have holidays at the same time. If they do something else they may not have your holidays and you might only get to see each other at the weekend – if this is the case you could work the majority of your holidays and have most weekends off.

How you spend your weekends will depend on how you use these holidays. But don't forget, as much as you would like to forget: there are things that will have to be done on the odd weekend – that lesson you have to change, those resources you have decided to use and haven't yet made. Things come up in this profession all the time, so be prepared to give up some of your free time.

By the way, there will be those teachers who tell you they never work on the weekend, they never work in the holidays and they still seem to get all their work done. Their secret? They've been doing it longer!

Life as a teacher

DEALING WITH STRESS

Different people have different symptoms of stress: some stop eating, some stop sleeping, some get irritable and some (me) eat chocolate.

Today schools have an obligation to teachers who find the work–life balance difficult to achieve. Many have courses on how to deal with stress, and I would certainly recommend them. There are also practical things you should do if you start to feel that things are getting on top of you.

Most new teachers start having problems when work gets too much: they have this set of books to mark and this photocopying to do and these lessons they are worrying about, and suddenly they have headaches and dizzy spells. As a new teacher you need to organize your time. You can't do everything at the same time and this can panic new teachers. So:

○ Make a list in order of importance of what needs to be done and do one thing at a time.
○ Look at what you can pass on to others, e.g. a departmental administrator or a teaching assistant can take care of some of the smaller tasks such as photocopying.
○ If things do get out of control tell your head of department and they should help you in any way they can.

Everybody will sometimes feel they have no life outside school but teachers I fear are the worst at this. You get to Monday morning and you can't work out where Saturday or Sunday went, but by now you have another week ahead of you and you know next weekend will disappear just as quickly. Before you know it you are eating, drinking and sleeping school and you have no life. This makes for a very unhappy, tired and ineffectual teacher.

There is no need for it. Granted, often evenings disappear – I have rehearsals until late and by the time I get home I can just about fall into bed. However as a teacher you do get weekends, so use them. Oh, I know what you're going to say: well if I don't have school work I have to clean the house, do the washing and the ironing. STOP! From 1 September you will start on a reasonable salary. On Saturday mornings, take your clothes to the launderette and get a service wash. Costs me £5.50, wash, dry and iron. Next, hire a cleaner, once a week, £25 a week, and suddenly you have a weekend. Get out! Too many people stay in – instead climb mountains, take long walks . . . well OK then, have a nice meal, see friends or go to the cinema, but you get my meaning.

BEAUTY SLEEP

I can't function on two hours' sleep. I definitely can't teach and I wouldn't suggest you try. Teaching is exhausting enough without adding late nights, so be sensible about what time you get to bed. I'm not saying you should be in bed by 8. You should make sure you have some sort of evening otherwise you will feel that all you do is go to school, come home, go to bed, get up and go to school, again and again. Don't do this – you should have some time out at the end of the day to forget about school and planning and marking, otherwise you'll find yourself lying awake thinking about work. There are a number of ways to do this and it depends on the individual. You might want to go out for a walk or a swim. You might want to go out for the evening or just settle on the sofa, in front of the TV with a hot drink or a good book. Do anything that you can to come down from the whirlwind that is school, but be a Cinderella and be in bed by midnight.

I really believe that a good morning can make for a good day, and it is something not enough teachers think about, especially new ones. It's simple: if you get up late and are rushing about trying to get your bag together and then running out the door without breakfast you will be tired and irritable by the time you get to school, and you'll be hungry by period one.

Have a real structure to your morning. Get up in plenty of time so you are not rushing. Get things ready the night before, like your lunch and bag, and sit down and have a proper breakfast. Breakfast is one of those meals so many people don't have, and their excuses are endless. People say they don't have time – get up earlier. Some say they just can't eat before 9 o'clock – well, train yourself. Oh, and by breakfast I don't mean last night's pizza. Have something that will give you energy: cornflakes, toast, anything sensible.

Also think about your trip to school. I know teachers who mark books on the way to school or attempt to do the washing up in the morning, or plan lessons while in the car. Don't – it is not worth it. Listen to some music, read a chapter of a book and start the day in a relaxing way. After all it's a safe bet that your day will get hectic all on its own, it won't need you rushing around and getting hot and bothered before you've even got to school.

START YOUR DAY THE RIGHT WAY

There are some teachers who come every day in a suit but if you are in a subject where that isn't possible I would always suggest you have at least one really smart suit that you feel good in. This can be used for a number of things: parents' evenings, school performance evenings, and sometimes if you have a difficult group wearing a suit when you are teaching them can often make you feel more confident.

Think carefully about what you wear to class. Schools are notorious places for being too hot or too cold, and usually are both in the same week. They are also messy places, ink can fly in any class and if you do anything creative then you can be covered from head to foot by break. Therefore I would always wear a layer of clothes you can take off when you are hot and pile on when you are cold. I would also recommend that you take a change of clothes. It can be difficult to feel relaxed in front of a class when you have spilt your lunch all over your white shirt.

Lastly on the clothes issue, white is a teacher's worst colour. It shows up sweat patches, and don't forget you do have to write on the board. One little mark on it looks dreadful. It is just not worth the risk.

I can remember saying a million times in my lifetime before my teaching career 'I'm tired'. Take it from me, you don't know the meaning of the word tired until you have started your first year.

Some people go on and on about how much time students have and how new teachers get such an easy deal because they get a reduced timetable. Yes, new teachers do get a reduced timetable, but that is because they need it. Everything is new to you and is harder. Even simple things like preparing your resources will take you longer because, newsflash, it's new to you. You will spend more energy on thinking and worrying about classes than anyone in the school; you will spend more time on lessons, reports, everything, therefore by the time your last term comes around you will be on your knees. For the first two weeks of my first summer holiday I slept an average of 13 hours a night. I was tired. The key to success? Look after yourself.

12 REPORTS, 2 PARENTS' EVENINGS, 4 MEETINGS, 70 BOOKS TO MARK AND IT'S ONLY WEDNESDAY

I'VE GOT A HEADACHE, I'M COUGHING AND SNEEZING – I'LL GO TO SCHOOL

Going to work when feeling dreadful is a teacher thing. I'm sure of it. You could have the plague and you would still go in to school, teach and stay for the departmental meeting afterwards. It's pointless but a worry for new teachers especially because, as with lunches, you will have those teachers who tell you how they haven't taken a day sick in 40 years of teaching. Well, bully for them!

If you are ill there are several things you have to think about seriously. Firstly you work with children. They do not have fully developed immune systems and so by going to school with bugs spilling from you every time you sneeze you could end up passing it to the whole of Year 8. Though this would make for a quiet week it's not the best of ideas. Next your colleagues: a school can deal with one or two teachers off but not half or all of your department! Don't forget you often work in close proximity with other teachers, particularly if your department office is small, as ours is. As my head of department said to me when I was ill, the school does go on without you: so take the time off.

However, work is a major worry for people when they are sick. You have to call the school and give your work over the phone. Make sure you have a back-up plan. Put together a little folder with work in it for each year and class that can be done as a one-off, or a small unit that can be done at any time, maybe work on basic skills, or do something fun. Have crosswords and word searches up your sleeve or even get them to design their own – these can be subject-specific to any lesson.

One last piece of advice on this. A major mistake many teachers make is returning to work too early. Insurance for cover teachers comes into effect after two days, therefore you can feel no guilt about taking that extra day to make sure you are completely well again.

Fact: teachers get time for lunch. Fact: teachers often don't take lunch. Lunchtime is when you do that bit of photocopying you forgot to do earlier. It's when you make that phone call to the person who is lucky enough to leave work at 4 and you know you won't be home until 5. It's the time when you see this pupil or that pupil because their coursework is a week late. Either way, lunch comes and goes and it often doesn't include food. I once ate my cup of soup while I was trying to model physical theatre during Year 7 drama club. Trust me, it was a messy experience. Plenty of teachers will tell you heroic stories of how they live on the odd chocolate bar and water for the full five days. It doesn't make them more effective teachers so don't sacrifice the one thing that could get you through the day.

Make sure you take some time to sit down and have lunch. Even if you can only manage fifteen minutes, it will do. A good trick is to have a hot meal, a baked potato or something that has to be eaten sitting at a table, and try not to eat rubbish – proper food gives you far more energy. The nurse at your local medical centre can give you advice on this.

A MARS BAR AND WATER MAKE LUNCH

LOOKING AFTER YOURSELF ALL DAY

A teacher's day can be very long and so you need to take care of yourself.

YOUR FEET

As a teacher you will walk miles in a week – up stairs, down stairs, along corridors, across playgrounds and fields, not to mention how long you'll stand up when in class – few teachers are able to teach effectively sitting down. Therefore having a really comfortable pair of shoes is invaluable. This doesn't necessarily mean an expensive pair. I have gone through more shoes since I've been in school than at any other time in my life, so have a pair for school and only for school.

YOUR VOICE

As a teacher your main tool is your voice. Teachers stretch their voices to the limit, particularly those who like to shout. Apart from the fact that shouting doesn't work with pupils, it is also bad for your voice. Let's face it, you need your voice, so don't shout unless it is really necessary. Warm up your voice before a full day of teaching, I sing in the shower to warm mine up. Also be aware of the smallest tickle. As soon as you feel any irritation gargle with Aspirin and drink lemon and honey. Always carry a bottle of water. It is very easy running around school to get dehydrated. It's bad for you and your voice. There is nothing more embarrassing than croaking out your lesson objectives or suddenly getting violent coughs in front of Year 10.

YOUR BACK

All teachers put their backs through hell, day in, day out, with uncomfortable chairs, reaching for the board and carrying piles of books. The first thing to do is to find out where your caretakers live and make friends with them. I find biscuits usually work – even better are chocolate ones. These wonderful people will help you by carrying heavy equipment such as large televisions. (And for when things do go wrong, find your nearest massage parlour.)

A HEADACHE

A teacher's worst enemy is a headache. Schools are noisy places and you can't teach when your head is thumping away. So keep a store of painkillers at school. However, a warning: schools have particular rules about drugs. *Never* give them to children, and make sure you keep them locked away.

MAKING MISTAKES

The greatest fear of teachers new to the profession is of the mistakes they might make. Let me tell you the ending right now – you will make mistakes, lots of them, but that is because you are new to the job. If you do make a mistake don't panic! Learn from it, work out what went wrong and why, apologize for it and then move on. I made plenty of mistakes – including getting names of senior management wrong, spelling important words wrongly on the board and even falling asleep on the train and missing my stop! The best way to get over it is to be humble, bribe people with chocolates and make plenty of notes. To be honest you will always make mistakes, all teachers do – even those who have been in the profession for years, so don't stress yourself.

There will be one day where you will want to give up. You have one bad class after the other, a report you forgot that was due in yesterday and it will seem as if everyone is on your back. You will get home upset and tired and you won't be able to think about going into school the next day. This is the day you'll say, I don't want to be a teacher. I think I said it about a dozen times in the first term! Don't just get miserable about this. Talk to someone – it might be that you go home and go on about it to your partner or housemate. Explain your day to them and how you feel, and that in itself will make you feel better.

However it might be that when you get up the next day to go to school you can hardly bear the thought of it and end up feeling sick with a headache that won't go away. This is a sure sign that it is something a bit more serious than just a bad day. Look at your lessons, change any really stressful ones and give yourself a bit of space, and then at the first possible moment speak to your head of department or the head of new teachers. Be honest about needing help, it happens to us all.

THOSE DAYS WHEN YOU CAN'T TEACH

There are those wonderful jobs where on a day when you are just not up to it you can go in, close the door, sit in front of a computer, talk to no one and just wait until home time. I fantasize about jobs like that. But teaching just isn't one of them. Every day you have to go in and have to perform. Well, kind of. There is a way round it. There will be those days, often at the end of term, when you are tired, when the children are tired, and an outstanding lesson is just beyond you. Give yourself a break and prepare for the worst. Have a selection of lessons that are one-offs or small schemes of work of two or three lessons that the pupils can do mostly unaided and which have little or no marking involved.

For instance, have them design posters or a leaflet. These could be for anything: it might be you're doing *Romeo and Juliet* and you have them do a poster for a performance of it. Or maybe you want them to do a leaflet on safety in chemistry labs. You can also link these lessons to the start of a new scheme of work: have them research the topic, such as Shakespeare's life or some historical event. They could do this in the library or on the Internet. There is also of course the video lesson – if, for example, you've been doing *Oliver Twist*, show them the video. This does not make you a bad teacher, it makes you a realistic one. It will give you the time you need to recover yourself a bit and get you through the rest of the year.

One of the major problems teachers have is that they take their work home with them. I don't mean marking or lesson planning, but the stresses and annoyances of the day. Worrying about things at home makes it impossible to rest, which means you are tired the next day and likely to have bad things happen all over again. Teachers are not great at sharing what has happened, but you must. This is more than just passing the buck or asking for help – it's you sitting down and telling someone about your day. It might be a friend, partner or even another teacher. It will make you feel so much better and you'll be able to let things go far more easily.

SHARING YOUR DAY

TALKING SHOP

Schools are wonderful places for socializing opportunities – your school will probably organize regular outings, as will your department, and this is a lovely way to make friends with your department. However, teachers are notorious for talking shop. You go out and you talk about pupils, curriculum, exams and senior management. To some extent there is nothing wrong with this and it happens with any job; sharing ideas and notes can help you as a teacher but it doesn't help you switch off. I find myself talking shop even with my friends who aren't teachers but have children of their own. This means you don't stop and can be really boring for people who aren't into education. So listen to yourself, and when you realize you have just pulled apart the entire curriculum, talk about something new.

The eternal student

COURSES

Teaching is one of those professions that is forever changing, particularly thanks to the government that keeps coming up with brilliant new initiatives, which to be honest many teachers find difficult to keep a handle on! Ideas about education change all the time. The ideas fashionable in the 1960s were very different from how it is now perceived. Sometimes we think children need freedom, at other times we think they need positive discipline, sometimes they need targets and at other times they need grades.

Therefore you need to keep up with all the new buzz words. The best way to do this is to go on courses as these will give you up-to-date information and ideas and practical advice. They are also an excellent way to review knowledge that you may have skimmed over in your course. I found myself having to teach A-level theatre studies and was unsure about the technicalities of it so I went on a course for teachers 'new to A-level teaching' by Keynote Education, www.keynote.org.uk. It was wonderful. Keynote runs a number of courses all over the country and they are very practical with excellent ideas. The course took me through each different specification and focused on what the examiners were looking for. Your head of department will get sent lots of course information so ask them to pass it your way and tell them what you might be looking for.

Most teachers will specialize in a section of their subject, e.g. English teachers might specialize in 18th-century literature, drama teachers might specialize in technical theatre, and so on. However, most teachers do have to teach the whole curriculum and this can be very daunting for a new teacher who would rather teach something they are secure in. You should see this as an opportunity not only to learn a new topic but also to see it from the pupils' point of view, sections you find difficult to grasp the pupils will also find difficult. Think about how you end up understanding it and you're half-way to teaching it to others.

It's also worth asking a more experienced teacher how they teach the topic; maybe you can observe one of the lessons they do, or borrow some of their resources. Use the experience of others and be open to the fact that they might also ask for your input at some point.

If all else fails, talk to the teacher in charge of teacher training. The school is obliged to keep training you – say you need a course on poetry or Russian history, you should ask to be sent on such courses, but get these requests in at the beginning of term as the funding does run out!

YOUR SUBJECT, YOUR LEARNING

VIDEOING YOURSELF

It's very difficult when you are teaching to be aware of what you are doing right or wrong. Therefore I would suggest you video yourself a couple of times during the year. This allows you to look at every aspect of your teaching – from what you say to how you stand. Pick different groups to do this with: a very good group and one you're having problems with. It is also worth watching this video with your mentor – you might find you are doing some surprising things. I had one very difficult group and when I watched myself on tape I realized I spent a lot of time with my arms crossed, a very defensive position for a teacher and not at all a good idea.

It's also worth making targets for yourself and then videoing yourself a couple of weeks later – have you in fact met your target? If not, try and try again.

Teachers hate doing this. It's ironic – we ask pupils to do it all the time. As a professional you should always be assessing yourself. You are expected during your first year to constantly assess yourself and you will be expected to set (and meet) targets. Everyone else will assess you and it looks good for you if you are taking an active role in this process.

It's very difficult to be honest. You can make excuses: you had a bad day, the resources got mixed up, or it was raining and the pupils always behave worse when they're wet. But in truth when you have a bad lesson there is always something to assess and change. Think about:

o What areas do you need to improve on?
o What did go wrong?
o Which pupils were leading the bad behaviour?
o Most importantly, how did you react under stress: did you shout, go red, play with your hair?

All of this should be observed and changed for the better. To show this active involvement, keep a record of your tapes, show them to your mentor and discuss the findings with other new teachers.

SELF-ASSESSMENT

KEEP READING

The fact that you are reading this book means that you already read around your job but it is really important in developing the pool of information you will need to be an effective teacher to keep reading all through your career.

There are books on every part of teaching. Sure, those on behaviour are the most popular but there are books on everything, for example the 'Red Hot Starters' series published by Letts Educational has books on great starters for subjects such as mathematics, science, English, ICT and DT.

It's easy when you find a writer you like only to read what they publish, but remember, every class is different and strategies that work with one group won't always work with another one, therefore reading a variety of books by different people is your best way of finding strategies that work for different groups. Also make sure you read books that have up-to-date theories, especially on behaviour.

As well as books and courses there are a lot of television programmes about teaching, from the BBC's *Head of the Class* to documentaries about failing schools. All these can help give you an insight not only into how other teachers deal with problems but also what other schools are like. If you were lucky you may have had two very good schools in your training year and may then go to your new school thinking it's out of control. Watching programmes on schools that really are struggling can put your problems into perspective. They are definitely worth a look.

OTHER SOURCES OF INFORMATION

ADMIT YOUR WEAKNESSES

We all have weaknesses, especially as new teachers. It might be that you can't write on the board neatly, or that you find revision lessons difficult, or perhaps you don't know how to cater for pupils with SEN. Whatever it is, it will often be a great source of stress for a new teacher.

The only way to deal with it is to admit it and work on a strategy to overcome the problem. If it is something to do with SEN or gifted and talented, go and see a member of that department and they will be able to give you some information on it. There are courses for these areas which may also be helpful.

If it's a smaller thing like writing on the board, find ways round it, go into work early so you can spend time on it, put the exercises on an OHP, or do handouts. You can also get the pupils to write on the board instead. There are ways round most problems – you just need to think about it!

Many people can often think of 101 things they are bad at but seem to struggle to find one thing they are good at. This is silly – everyone is good at something and although these talents might not seem to be linked to your subject in any way they can in fact be used to make a subject clearer, more interesting and easier for you. After all, lessons are at their best when the teacher is comfortable and having fun.

If you can use a computer in a creative way then do so. Come up with an interactive quiz, *Who wants to be a millionaire*-style as a plenary to your chemistry lesson. Maybe you have been testing them on the periodic table. Ask the question 'what is the symbol for iron?' and have four answers. You could even put a pupil in 'the hot seat' so they have an audience to ask.

If you're a history teacher who likes drama and find it hard to teach what it was like in the Middle Ages, have them act it out or come in medieval dress, and if you are fabulous in the kitchen for religious education cook a kosher meal, they'll love eating it and so will you!

MAKE YOUR STRENGTHS CLEAR

One year down, another 44 (at least) to go

July is a very strange month, so don't panic if things start to fall apart, sixth formers turn up less and less, homework either isn't done at all or is given in on a scrap of paper, even staff seem to be talking more about next year than anything else. Not that you can relax just yet. Try your best to hold on to your boundaries and expectations while also wrapping up work: don't let your class go for the summer not having finished an essay or a novel. Plan ahead. Discount the last week of term because you'll have sports days, awards days and any other days your school can think of.

Most importantly for you, this is the time that you will be talking to your mentor about your year and about passing (if you've got this far you've passed).

Next, focus on your six-week break. July has come and the relief of your first year ending will be enormous. You will be able to stay in bed until noon, go to bed late and stay out on a school night. One of the great things about being a teacher is the long summer – enjoy it. Sleep, have time off, go on holiday, and while you're doing all this you are still getting paid!

So, do you still want to be a teacher?

You must be thinking, what? After all the hard work, the sweat, the tears, you're asking do I still want to do this? But seriously, life is too short to be in a job you hate. So if the thought of crowded corridors and choruses of 'Miss, Miss' or 'Sir, Sir' gives you nightmares and makes your skin crawl then maybe teaching is not for you. You must start thinking about this before the end of the year. It is not unheard of at the end of the first year for teachers to move on to a different job and there is no shame in it.

Your training cannot really prepare you for the job. It is only in this first year where you really learn what the job is and it's not for everyone. Staying in a job you hate won't make you a good teacher, nor will it make you a happy one. So think carefully, is this job the one you want?

Don't forget after your first year you are a teacher. You can always come back to it, you could do supply for a little extra money so this doesn't have to be the end, but nor does it have to be for the rest of your life.

DO YOU STILL WANT TO BE A TEACHER?

ARE YOU IN THE RIGHT SCHOOL FOR YOU?

Many new teachers make mistakes in their first school and so prefer to move schools for their second year. You must first check the latest you can hand in your resignation and of course you have to start the process again of finding another job. However you may find that during your first year this is a bit much. You will have just settled, you know the teachers, the school rules, the pupils, and the thought of starting again this early on is very difficult. I would think very carefully about this before you do it.

Ask yourself:

o Does this school have the ethos I'm looking for?
o Am I teaching the subject I wanted (you might have gone for an English job with a little drama and find you are teaching too much drama).
o Have you fitted in with the staff and the school system?
o Are you well supported?
o Is the catchment area right for you?
o Is the location right? If you are spending too much time travelling you might want to move to a school nearer your home.
o And most importantly, are you happy, do you enjoy going to school every day?

If you do decide to move on you have an advantage. You have been through the interview process recently, so you'll be more aware of what questions they will ask and what sort of lesson you might do. However, they will ask you why you want to move on so early. Be careful how you answer this question.

Do say:

○ You're moving to be closer to home.
○ You want to teach A-level and haven't had the opportunity.
○ You want to work with smaller or larger numbers.
○ You want more diverse students, e.g. it might be the school has a larger SEN intake, maybe you feel you could really support special needs and would like the challenge.
○ You want to try a really different school to expand your knowledge.

Don't say:

○ It's because you hated the previous school.
○ That you didn't like the pupils.

If you decide to stay put you will find that you can make your second year far easier. You know the pupils, the schemes of work, you should already have all your lesson plans and resources. Spend some of the summer reviewing these – what worked, what didn't? Spend time too on new resources and new ideas, all of which will be work that you don't have to do during the year.

THIS TIME YOU KNOW WHAT'S COMING

The average length of time a person stays in teaching is only three years.

Teaching is still one of the hardest, most stressful jobs going. It forever changes with new ideas; schools are a constant conveyer belt with new pupils all the time. Therefore all the points in this book about learning, taking care of yourself, etc., do in fact remain true for your entire career. Teaching will never get easier but at the same time will never lose its importance.

THE REST OF YOUR LIFE AS A TEACHER

AND FINALLY . . .

Think carefully before rushing into extra responsibilities in your second year. Lots of new teachers start to look at options such as tutoring or heading up a Key Stage. Although you will find your second year a lot easier there will be things in your second year that you didn't have to do in your first year, e.g. exam marking, faculty paperwork, etc. Your mentor/head of department will have taken a lot of the strain from you, more than you will have known about. They can't do this forever because you'd never learn, so be prepared and don't take on too much for your second year – after all you are still relatively new at this.